MRJC
02/18

Wildebeest Migration

by Grace Hansen

Abdo
ANIMAL MIGRATION
Kids

abdopublishing.com

Published by Abdo Kids, a division of ABDO, P.O. Box 398166, Minneapolis, Minnesota 55439.

Copyright © 2018 by Abdo Consulting Group, Inc. International copyrights reserved in all countries. No part of this book may be reproduced in any form without written permission from the publisher.

Printed in the United States of America, North Mankato, Minnesota.

052017

092017

THIS BOOK CONTAINS
RECYCLED MATERIALS

Photo Credits: iStock, Shutterstock

Production Contributors: Teddy Borth, Jennie Forsberg, Grace Hansen

Design Contributors: Dorothy Toth, Laura Mitchell

Publisher's Cataloging in Publication Data

Names: Hansen, Grace, author.

Title: Wildebeest migration / by Grace Hansen.

Description: Minneapolis, Minnesota : Abdo Kids, 2018 | Series: Animal migration
   | Includes bibliographical references and index.

Identifiers: LCCN 2016962368 | ISBN 9781532100338 (lib. bdg.) |
   ISBN 9781532101021 (ebook) | ISBN 9781532101571 (Read-to-me ebook)

Subjects: LCSH: Gnus--Juvenile literature. | Wildebeest migration--Juvenile
   literature.

Classification: DDC 599.64--dc23

LC record available at http://lccn.loc.gov/2016962368

Table of Contents

Wildebeests

Wildebeests live in the grassy **plains** of Africa. Many are found in the **Serengeti**. The Serengeti is in Tanzania and Kenya.

4

Wildebeests eat plants.

Grass is their favorite food.

Nearly 500,000 calves are born in January and February of each year. They are born in the southern plains of the Serengeti in Tanzania.

9

Following the Rain

Grass is harder to find in March. The rains that grew the grass moved west. As many as 1.5 million wildebeests must move too.

Wildebeests move west until June or July. The **herd** comes to the Grumeti River in the central **Serengeti**.

Crossing rivers can be scary for wildebeests. Crocodiles are often waiting. But the herd must keep moving to find grass.

15

By July and August, the herd is usually near the Mara River. They cross the river into Kenya. This is the farthest north they travel.

Heading South Again

The **herd** remains in Kenya until around October. By November, they have made their way south again.

The **herd** rests in December. They have traveled nearly 1,000 miles. Most have made it back to where they started. The herd will make the same journey in a few months.

21

Wildebeest Migration Routes

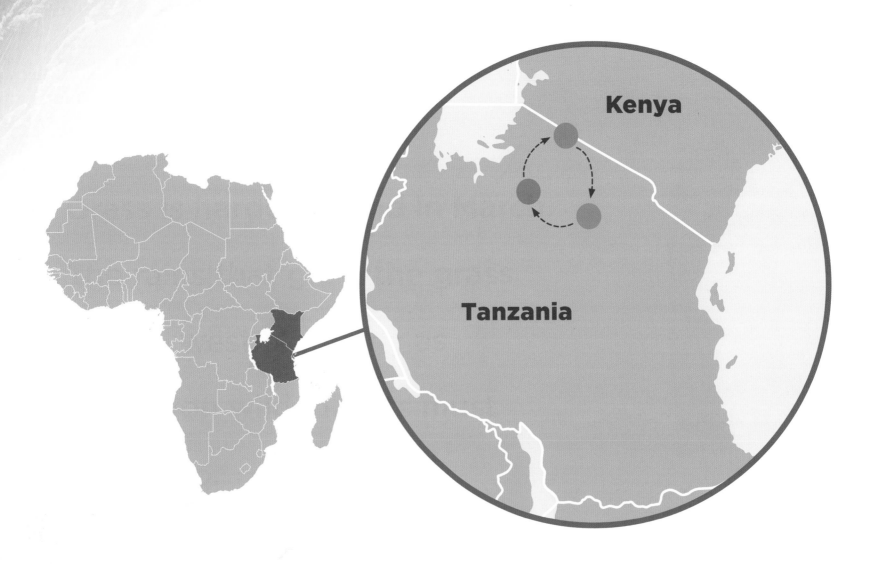

● June Home   ● September Home   ● January Home   ◄----► Route

Glossary

calf – a baby wildebeest.

herd – a large group of wildebeests that live, feed, and travel together.

plain – a large area of flat land with grasses and few trees.

Serengeti – a vast plain in Tanzania and Kenya (the portion in Kenya is known as Maasai Mara) where many large mammals and birds live.

Index

abdokids.com

Use this code to log on to abdokids.com and access crafts, games, videos and more!

Abdo Kids Code:
AWK0338